W9-ALM-485

TOP 10 FOOTBALL RECEIVERS

Stew Thornley

SPORTS TOP 10

j 796.332
THO

ENSLOW PUBLISHERS, INC.

44 Fadem Rd.	P.O. Box 38
Box 699	Aldershot
Springfield, N.J. 07081	Hants GU12 6BP
U.S.A.	U.K.

DC RR

Library of Congress Cataloging-in-Publication Data

Thornley, Stew.
      Top 10 football receivers/Stew Thornley.
          p. cm. — (Sports Top 10)
      Includes index.
      ISBN 0-89490-607-0
      1. Wide receivers (Football)—United States—Biography— Juvenile literature.
  [1. Football players.] I. Title II. Title: Top ten football receivers. III. Series.
GV939.A1T48   1995
796.332—dc20   94-32062
                                                CIP
                                                AC

Printed in the United States of America

10 9 8 7 6 5 4 3 2 1

Photo Credits: Indianapolis Colts, p. 13; © 1994, Jerry Liebman Studio, Inc., p. 33; John
Biever, pp. 22, 25, 34, 37; New York Jets, pp. 26, 29; Photo by Scott Cunningham, p. 31,
Pittsburgh Steelers Football Club, pp. 42, 45; San Diego Historical Society, Union-
Tribune Collection, pp. 6, 9; Stiller Photos/Collection of Lee Lefebure, pp. 19, 21;
University of Wisconsin, pp. 15, 17; Vernon J. Biever, pp. 11, 39, 41.

Cover Photo: John Biever

Interior Design: Richard Stalzer

15195

CONTENTS

INTRODUCTION

THEY WERE ORIGINALLY CALLED ENDS—players at the end of the line who would go out for passes. Later the term flanker was used to describe a player in the backfield who went out for passes. Today they are all referred to as wide receivers.

They are the players who can quickly turn a game around or break it wide open. Even the best running backs average only around 5 yards per carry. But the receivers can get much more with a big catch. Highlight films of any football game are filled with the exploits of the graceful, high-flying pass catchers—running routes, using speed and cunning to get open, catching passes, and then running for more yards. That's a typical Sunday for a pass receiver in the National Football League (NFL).

Charley Sanders, a fine receiver for many years with the Detroit Lions, summed up his profession this way: "The easiest part of our business is catching the ball. The hard parts are getting open, being where you are supposed to be—and then holding on to the ball after you have caught it."[1]

Statistics can help narrow down the very best receivers of all time. How many passes have they caught? How many yards have they covered with those catches? But the numbers tell only part of the story. The impact that receivers have on football goes far beyond mere statistics.

The game has changed drastically over the years. In the early days of the NFL, a team's offense consisted mostly of running the ball. But as the forward pass became accepted, players emerged with the grace, speed, and toughness to venture out into the heart of the opposing team's defense to catch a pass and bring a long gain.

As more great quarterbacks have entered the league, more passes than ever before are being thrown—and caught.

Usually the highest paid players on a team are the quarterbacks, the ones who do the passing. But where would they be without a receiver at the other end? A "Top Ten" list could contain any combination of names, with so many great stars to choose from. Here is *my* list.

CAREER STATISTICS

Player	Seasons	Receptions	Yards	Average Yards Per Reception	Touchdowns
LANCE ALWORTH	11	542	10,266	18.9	85
RAYMOND BERRY	13	631	9,275	14.7	68
ELROY HIRSCH	12	387	7,029	18.2	60
DON HUTSON	11	488	7,991	16.4	99
STEVE LARGENT	14	819	13,089	16	100
DON MAYNARD	16	634	11,844	18.7	88
ART MONK	14	888	12,026	13.5	65
JERRY RICE	9	708	11,776	16.6	118
STERLING SHARPE	6	501	7,015	14	47
LYNN SWANN	9	336	5,462	16.3	51

LANCE ALWORTH

Lance Alworth makes one of his famous leaping catches. His deer-like acrobatic abilities earned him the nickname "Bambi".

LANCE ALWORTH

HIS NICKNAME SAID IT ALL: Bambi. Named after the Disney animal, Lance Alworth could jump like a deer and was just as quick. His ability to leap over defenders to make catches once caused a frustrated opponent to mutter, "What does he do? Train on a trampoline?"[1]

Alworth was a great all-around athlete in high school at Brookhaven, Mississippi. He made scholastic All-American in football, was a track star, and a baseball center fielder.

When he graduated, he decided to attend the University of Arkansas. He was an All-American running back and also led the country in returning punts his senior season.

When Alworth finished college in 1962, there were two major football leagues in operation: the older National Football League (NFL) and the American Football League (AFL), which was about to enter its third season. Alworth decided to go with the new league and the San Diego Chargers.

It wasn't as good as the NFL, but fans had to admit the AFL had some great players. Alworth quickly became the showpiece of the league. He was not a running back. He was the league's premier pass catcher. He was too small to stay in the backfield so he became a flanker.

He fit right in with his team's offense. Charger coach Sid Gillman relied on a passing game and Alworth became a major part of the attack. He helped to make the AFL exciting.

He also helped the San Diego Chargers make it to three straight AFL title games. In the first one, for the 1963 championship, Alworth caught a 48-yard touchdown pass in a 51-10 win over the Boston Patriots.

Catching passes in the middle of the field—instead of

near the sidelines where he could quickly duck out of bounds—caused Alworth to get banged up a lot. But he was durable. He played much of the 1966 season with broken bones in both hands. He also hurt his knee, which cut down on his speed. As a result, he relied more on elusive pass patterns to get open and make catches. Despite the injuries, Alworth led the AFL in all pass receiving categories that year and caught 73 passes—the most ever for him in a season.

When the AFL finally merged with the NFL following the 1969 season, Alworth held a healthy chunk of the AFL receiving records. In fact, in the Chargers' final AFL game ever, Alworth broke a long-standing record of Don Hutson's by catching a pass in his ninety-sixth consecutive game. He also led the league in receptions for the second straight year.

There was still glory ahead for Alworth. He became a member of the Dallas Cowboys in 1971. He played a more important role in blocking for the Cowboys.

Dallas, with its potent offense, won the National Football Conference (NFC) championship, giving Alworth a chance to play in the Super Bowl. He made the most of it.

The Cowboys were ahead, 3-0, with barely a minute left in the first half. They drove to the Miami Dolphins' seven-yard line, hoping they could get the ball into the end zone.

Alworth, lined up on the left side of the line, took off as the ball was snapped, turned toward the inside, then cut sharply back toward the corner of the field. Roger Staubach lofted a pass which Alworth, now free of his defender, grabbed for a touchdown. The Cowboys went on to win the game, 24-3.

Alworth played one more season before he retired. Perhaps no one had greater words to say than Charley Hennigan, another great pass catcher from the AFL, who said: "A player comes along once in a lifetime who alone is worth the price of admission. That player is Lance Alworth."[2]

LANCE ALWORTH

BORN: August 3, 1940.

HIGH SCHOOL: Brookhaven High School, Brookhaven, Mississippi.

COLLEGE: University of Arkansas.

PRO: San Diego Chargers, 1962-1970; Dallas Cowboys, 1971-1972.

RECORDS: Led AFL in all pass receiving categories, 1966.

HONORS: Inducted into Pro Football Hall of Fame in 1978.

Alworth makes another catch in the middle of the field and scrambles for yardage. His many injuries came in large part from catching passes in mid-field, away from the safety of the sidelines.

RAYMOND BERRY

ONLY A MINUTE-AND-A-HALF REMAINED in the fourth quarter as Raymond Berry stepped up to the line of scrimmage. His team, the Baltimore Colts, trailed the New York Giants, 16-13, in the 1958 NFL Championship Game. The Colts were on their own twenty-five-yard line, a long way from the Giants' end zone.

Just to get to this point, a chance to play for the NFL title, was a major achievement for Raymond Berry. He was not considered to be good enough for a pro career. Even the Colts, the team that signed him, didn't take him until the twentieth round of the college draft. Berry wasn't fast; in fact, one leg was shorter than the other. He also had poor eyesight and a bad back.

Berry used the skills he had to the best of his ability. He perfected a series of moves that helped him to shake off defenders and get open.

Berry's hard work and dedication paid off. He became the favorite receiver for the Colts' great quarterback, Johnny Unitas. In his third year with the Colts, he was determined to help them fight back and beat the Giants for the NFL championship title.

The ball was snapped and Berry took off downfield. As his defender backpedaled, Berry turned sharply toward the sidelines. Unitas' pass was already in the air and Berry hauled it in for a 25-yard gain. Another sideline pattern got him open, this time for a 16-yard pass reception. On the next play, Unitas again looked for Berry and found him at the twenty-one-yard line. On three passes from Unitas, Berry covered 54 yards.

RAYMOND BERRY

Raymond Berry was one of Pro-football's All-Time Leading Receivers during his thirteen year career.

The Colts were almost out of time, though. Instead of trying for a touchdown to win the game, they kicked a field goal that tied the score.

The tie was broken in overtime, the first ever played in the NFL. It was sudden-death overtime, meaning the first team to score wins. The Colts won a coin toss and got the ball first. They soon appeared stuck, however, as they faced a third down and 15 yards to go from their own thirty-six-yard line. Then Berry broke free from two defenders to catch a pass, running all the way to the Giants' forty-three-yard line before he was tackled. A run by halfback Alan Ameche brought the ball down to the twenty-yard line. The Colts were now close enough to kick a field goal that would win it. But Unitas wanted to get closer and decided on another pass to his favorite receiver. This time, Berry started toward the sideline, then darted back to the middle of the field where he plucked the pass out of the air for a 12-yard gain. A few plays later, Ameche rumbled into the end zone for a touchdown. This dramatic win by the Colts has been called the "Greatest Game Ever Played." On the two drives that counted most— one to tie the game and the other to win it—Raymond Berry caught five passes covering 87 yards.

Berry went on to many more great years with the Colts. He played in two more NFL title games with them and was named to the league's All-Pro team three times. Raymond Berry was inducted into the Pro Football Hall of Fame in 1973.

Tom Landry, coach of the Dallas Cowboys, said, "Raymond Berry was the guy who started moves in the NFL. He worked on and perfected those moves."[1]

RAYMOND BERRY

BORN: February 27, 1933.

HIGH SCHOOL: Paris High School, Paris, Texas.

COLLEGE: Southern Methodist University.

PRO: Baltimore Colts, 1955–1967.

RECORDS: Led NFL in receiving, 1958–1960.

HONORS: Pro Football Hall of Fame, 1973; NFL All-Pro Team, 3 times.

Following his playing days with the Baltimore Colts, Berry went on to coach several NFL teams.

ELROY HIRSCH

HE TURNED A BAD BREAK into good fortune. In the process, he thrilled fans and helped to popularize the long pass.

Elroy Hirsch had been an outstanding halfback at the University of Wisconsin in the early 1940s. He was most remembered, however, for his strange running style. Following a great run during his sophomore season, a reporter wrote, "Hirsch ran like a demented duck. His crazy legs were gyrating in six different directions all at the same time."[1] Forever after, Elroy Hirsch would be known as "Crazy Legs."

A teammate of Hirsch's in the professional ranks, Norm Van Brocklin, found another way to describe his running style: "You've heard of people who zig or zag. Well, Elroy also has a 'zog' and a couple of 'zugs.' "[2]

As a member of the Chicago Rockets of the All-American Football Conference, Hirsch had little success as a running back. In addition, his career was hampered by a number of frustrating injuries. The final injury, a fractured skull, made it seem that his playing days would be over.

Elroy Hirsch was determined to keep playing. He worked hard to recover. He ended up finding a new team, the Los Angeles Rams of the National Football League.

The Rams relied heavily on passing and wanted Hirsch to be part of that attack. But they already had a pair of outstanding ends. So Coach Joe Stydahar created a new position for Hirsch: flanker. Hirsch became the first back to be split wide and play primarily as a receiver.[3]

He used his natural speed, along with his unique running style, to develop into a great receiver. Hirsch often amazed people by catching up with passes that seemed overthrown.

ELROY HIRSCH

Hirsch earned his nickname, "Crazy Legs", after a reporter commented on his unique style of running. His legs appear to move in ways no one dreamed were possible.

Led by "Crazy Legs" Hirsch, the Rams won the National Football League title in 1951. Hirsch led the league with 66 receptions and 102 points scored. He set a new record for yards gained receiving and tied Don Hutson's mark of 17 touchdown catches in a season. Six of those touchdown catches were for 70 yards or more.

One of the most spectacular catches came during a mid-season game against the Chicago Bears. Not only did the Rams trail by two touchdowns, but they were backed up inside their own ten-yard line. Often a team in this situation will stick to the ground rather than risk throwing an interception deep in its own territory. But the Rams had Crazy Legs Hirsch and were willing to take a chance.

Hirsch took off at the snap and had reached full speed as he neared midfield. He looked up and saw that Bob Waterfield's long pass was sailing too far beyond him to catch. He sped up, reached out with his fingertips, and gathered the ball in without breaking stride. Hirsch glided the rest of the way for a 91-yard touchdown, a play that helped spark his team to a 42-17 win.

During the season, Hirsch had a touchdown reception of 81 yards and four more for at least 70 yards. For his efforts in 1951, Hirsch was named the Pro Player of the Year. During his career, which lasted through 1957, Hirsch averaged more than 18 yards per catch.

Although he was done playing, Crazy Legs Hirsch remained in the public spotlight. Hollywood made a movie of his career, *Crazy Legs—All-American.*

From 1969 to 1987, Hirsch also served as the athletic director at his alma mater, the University of Wisconsin.

Elroy Hirsch is best remembered for his work on the field. Hirsch was named the best flanker of football's first fifty years and was elected to the Football Hall of Fame in 1968.[4]

BORN: June 17, 1923.

HIGH SCHOOL: Wausau High School, Wausau, WI.

COLLEGE: University of Wisconsin and University of Michigan.

PRO: Chicago Rockets, 1946–1948; Los Angeles Rams, 1949–1957.

RECORDS: Most Yards Gained Receiving, 1951; Led NFL in all receiving categories, 1951.

HONORS: Pro Player of the Year, 1951; Pro Football Hall of Fame, 1968.

Hirsch was inducted into the College Football Hall of Fame in honor of his spectacular play-making abilities at Wisconsin and Michigan.

DON HUTSON

EVEN THOUGH HE WAS CONSIDERED too frail for football, Don Hutson helped to revolutionize the game.[1] With his blazing speed and sure hands, he played a major role in making the forward pass a weapon in the National Football League.

Hutson grew up in Pine Bluff, Arkansas, and was recruited by the University of Alabama along with Paul "Bear" Bryant, a star end for one of Pine Bluff's rival schools. While Bryant (who later coached the Alabama Crimson Tide for many years) quickly became a star, Hutson spent most of his first two seasons at Alabama on the bench.

He finally made the starting lineup the next year and set the stage for a memorable senior year. With Bryant and Hutson serving as targets for quarterback Dixie Howell, Alabama won all of its games and went to the Rose Bowl, where they defeated Stanford, 29-13. The final game of Hutson's college career also turned out to be one of his best. He had a 54-yard touchdown reception in the second quarter and scored on another pass in the fourth quarter, finishing the day with six catches for 154 yards.

One of the spectators at the Rose Bowl that day was Curly Lambeau, the coach of the Green Bay Packers. Although he shared the concern of others that Hutson was too small to play in the pros, Lambeau signed the "Alabama Antelope" to a contract with the Packers in 1935.

Hutson quickly justified Lambeau's faith in him. His first play in the pros, against the Chicago Bears, was a memorable one. The Bears gave little attention to the small rookie and Hutson made them pay for it. He got behind his defender,

DON HUTSON

Don Hutson led the NFL in receptions eight times. He led the league in interceptions once. He was a nine-time All-Pro for the Green Bay Packers.

caught a long pass from Arnie Herber at midfield, and sailed untouched down the field for an 83-yard touchdown.

In his second season, he set a league record with 34 receptions. He also helped the Packers to the NFL Title Game in which they beat the Boston Redskins, 21-6. Hutson caught a 43-yard touchdown pass from Herber to start the scoring. During his career, Hutson would win two more NFL championships with the Packers.

It wasn't a championship game that Hutson remembers best, however. In his final season, the Packers beat the Lions, 57-21. Hutson, who scored four touchdowns in one quarter, recalls how the wind helped his team that day. "With the wind with us, we'd throw these long passes and I was able to get down there under them. I think their defensive backs didn't think the ball would travel as far as it did. And sometimes, when we were throwing into the wind, I'd have to circle back like I was going for a lazy fly ball just as I did when I played center field. There was never another game quite like that, at least one that I played in."[2]

By the time he retired following the 1945 season, Hutson owned nearly all the league's pass receiving records. Most of those records have since been broken. Don Hutson was the man who set the standards of excellence for others to pursue.

Hutson had more than just speed. He developed an array of pass patterns and moves that made it virtually impossible for one defender to cover him.

Greasy Neale, a former star and coach, said, "Hutson is the only man I ever saw who can run in three different directions at the same time."[3]

DON HUTSON

BORN: January 31, 1913.

HIGH SCHOOL: Pine Bluff High School, Pine Bluff, Arkansas.

COLLEGE: University of Alabama.

PRO: Green Bay Packers, 1935-1945.

RECORDS: NFL receptions record, 34, 1935 (since broken).

HONORS: Pro Football Hall of Fame in 1963.

Hutson was named NFL Player of the Year twice in his career—once in 1941 and again in 1942.

STEVE LARGENT

After fourteen years with the Seattle Seahawks, Steve Largent retired as the all-time NFL leader in total passes caught (819) and in touchdown passes caught (100).

STEVE LARGENT

EVEN THOUGH HE LED THE nation in touchdown receptions two years in a row while at Tulsa University, Steve Largent wasn't in great demand by the pros. He wasn't very big or very fast. So Largent ended up with the Seattle Seahawks, a brand-new team in 1976. Expansion teams weren't expected to win many games, but Largent helped them to win some glory.

During the 1983 playoffs, Seattle played Miami for the right to advance to the AFC Championship Game. The Seahawks trailed with barely two minutes left and faced a third down on their own forty-two yard line. Largent hadn't yet caught a pass, but with the game on the line, he got open for a catch good for 16 yards. Then on the next play, he raced down the right sideline, cut in and then quickly back out. He caught the ball for a 40-yard gain and set up the touchdown that gave the Seahawks the biggest win in their history.

Throughout his career, Largent made up for his lack of speed by working on his pass patterns. He had the ability to change direction quickly. Largent's success also came from his ability to concentrate on the ball and block out distractions—even the sound of footsteps of a defender about to crash into him.

It was this type of concentration that helped Largent to stay focused on what he wanted to do, even as he went through a lot of turmoil and change as a youngster in Oklahoma. His parents divorced and his mother married a man whose job forced the family to move several times.

Having to make new friends all of the time is a difficult task for anyone. It was especially hard for Largent, who didn't find it easy to fit in with the crowd. But he did find a home on the football field. At the age of fourteen, he tried out for the football team at Putnam High School in Oklahoma City. He started out at running back but fell flat. He had more success when he moved in with the receivers.

Football became something for Largent to cling to as his home life was becoming tougher to deal with.

Largent found other areas besides football to help stabilize his life. One was a girlfriend, Terry Bullock, who eventually became his wife. Another was a Christian faith that remains strong within Largent, his wife, and their children to this day.

He became a star in high school and went on to further greatness in college. Even so, he had to prove himself again in the professional ranks. Without any complaints, he did just that.

Although he became one of the greatest receivers in the history of the game, Largent was also one of the most modest. It was his usual manner to downplay his accomplishments. Many of Largent's greatest praises came from those who played against him. "He's the most deceptive receiver in football," said Mike Haynes, a cornerback for the Raiders who spent many frustrating Sundays trying to keep up with Largent.[1] Opponents who spent many frustrating Sundays trying to defend him knew how good he was.

Largent played through 1989 and finished his career as the all-time leader in receptions, yards receiving, and touchdowns (the only player besides Don Hutson to be number one in all three categories at the same time). He also set a record by catching a pass in 177 straight games. In his unspectacular but steady way, Steve Largent gave character and brought respect to a brand-new team.

STEVE LARGENT

BORN: September 28, 1954.

HIGH SCHOOL: Putnam High School, Oklahoma City, Oklahoma.

COLLEGE: Tulsa University.

PRO: Seattle Seahawks, 1976–1989.

RECORDS: Retired as all-time Career Leader in Receptions, Yards Receiving, and Touchdowns; Records number of games catching a pass (177 straight).

HONORS: All-Pro 3 times.

Largent set a record for catching a pass in 177 straight games.

DON MAYNARD

In his fifteen years in the league, Don Maynard was one of the all-time NFL leaders in receiving yards.

DON MAYNARD

HE WAS ON THE RECEIVING end of many of Joe Namath's passes but was also a star with the New York Jets long before Namath came along.

Don Maynard started his career with the New York Giants as a running back but played only five games with them in 1958. After a season in the Canadian Football League, Maynard returned to New York. This time it wasn't with the Giants, but with the New York Titans (later known as the Jets) in the first year of the American Football League. By then, Maynard was no longer a running back.

Maynard quickly became one of the premier receivers in the new league, catching 72 passes for more than twelve hundred yards in 1960. He wasn't the fastest player, and he sometimes frustrated his coaches by not sticking to planned pass patterns.

One of the biggest catches Maynard ever made came from Joe Namath in the 1968 AFL Championship Game. The Jets trailed Oakland by three points in the fourth quarter and had the ball on their own thirty-two yard line. Maynard raced down the sideline on a deep pattern. With a defensive back on his tail, Maynard saw that Namath's pass was falling short. As the defender tried to stop, Maynard wheeled around, came back for the ball, and grabbed it just before it hit the ground. He was finally tackled on the Oakland six-yard line. Moments later, he caught another pass, this one in the end zone to win the game for the Jets and send them to the Super Bowl. It was Maynard's second touchdown of the day. In all, he had six catches for 118 yards.

The roughness of the AFL championship game had left

Maynard with an injured leg. The Jets' opponents for the Super Bowl, the Baltimore Colts, didn't think Maynard would be much of a threat in the big game.

Early in the game, Namath and Maynard went for the long bomb. The ball ended up just out of Maynard's reach, but the close call caused the Colts to pay more attention to him the rest of the game. As a result, George Sauer, one of the other Jets' receivers was able to haul in eight passes from Namath. "While they were looking at Maynard," said Jets' assistant coach Clive Rush, "Joe was passing to Sauer."[1] Although he didn't catch a pass in the Super Bowl the following week, Maynard was still a factor with just his presence.

During his playing days, Maynard was known as a renegade. He was a free spirit who looked out of place in New York City with his cowboy boots. He also let his hair grow long and had sideburns well before they were in style.

Standing out from the crowd was Maynard's way of doing things. It served him well off the field and certainly added to his flair on the field.

In 1969 he went over the 10,000 yards receiving. He was the first player ever to reach that level. Fifty times in his career he had more than 100 yards receiving in a game, another record. Don Maynard was elected to the Football Hall of Fame in 1987.

Weeb Ewbank, who took over as Jets' coach in 1963, said, "He's deceptive. He has a gait that makes him look like he's coasting and then he turns it on, goes into overdrive, and leaves you there. He just explodes."[2]

DON MAYNARD

BORN: January 25, 1937.

HIGH SCHOOL: Colorado City (Texas) High School.

COLLEGE: Texas Western University.

PRO: New York Giants, 1958; Hamilton Tiger Cats, 1959; New York
Jets, 1960-1972; St. Lous Cardinals, 1973.

RECORDS: Career Record in Receiving Yards (over 10,000, no longer
a record); Career record for more than 100 yards receiving
in a game (50 times).

HONORS: Pro Football Hall of Fame, 1987.

Maynard was the first player to ever gain over 10,000 yards receiving
in his career.

Art Monk

IT WAS A MONDAY NIGHT GAME in October, 1992. Art Monk went into motion to his right as the quarterback barked out signals. At the snap of the ball, Monk took off upfield. He turned sharply to his right in time to catch the ball for a 10-yard gain. There was nothing flashy about the play but it was enough to bring the fans to their feet for a standing ovation.

The catch was the 820th of Monk's career, making him the all-time leader in pass receptions. The fact that the record-breaker was hardly the stuff of highlight films is appropriate. That's not the way Monk operates.

Joe Gibbs, who coached Monk for most of his years with the Washington Redskins, said, "He is not your typical receiver, who goes out there and runs patterns in air and space and catches balls."

Gibbs summed up the type of receiver Art Monk is: steady but not spectacular. Monk's never been afraid to venture into the middle of the field, where he's sure to get hit after making a catch. Despite this, he'll be remembered as an extremely durable player—playing nearly every down and rarely coming out of a game.

Monk was a track star in high school in White Plains, New York, but he had his sights set on similar success in football. The speed that made him stand out on the track aided him on the football field as well. However, it wasn't until he was at Syracuse University that the hard work began to show. He emerged as an outstanding receiver and also caught the eyes of pro scouts with some fine punt returns.

He was a first-round draft pick of the Washington

ART MONK

Art Monk's ability to make "big catches" in the "big games" has earned him the honor of being one of the all-time NFL leaders in receiving yards.

Redskins in 1980 and was a member of three Super Bowl championship teams with the Redskins. Monk's greatest season came in 1984 when he set an NFL record (since broken by Sterling Sharpe) by catching 106 passes. He also had 1,372 yards receiving, the highest total he ever achieved in his career.

Although he's never scored a touchdown in a Super Bowl, Monk has made some big catches in helping the Redskins to victory. He had a 40-yard reception in a 42-10 win over Denver in Super Bowl XXII. Four years later, he caught seven passes for 106 yards in a win over Buffalo. (It appeared he finally had his long-awaited touchdown in that game. He caught a ball in the end zone for an apparent touchdown. However, instant replay—which at the time could be used to overrule officials' on-field calls—showed that one of his feet was out of bounds when he made the catch.)

Monk has been a model of consistency in his career. That trait doesn't lead to a lot of attention but that's fine with him. Art Monk has made his achievements in his own quiet way. According to Joe Gibbs, "Art's the strongest outside receiver I have ever coached, and he has caught a lot of balls inside and taken the hit."[1]

ART MONK

BORN: December 5, 1957.

HIGH SCHOOL: White Plains, New York.

COLLEGE: Syracuse University.

PRO: Washington Redskins, 1980–1993; New York Jets, 1994– .

RECORDS: All-time Leader in Pass Receptions (888 through 1993).

HONORS: NFL All-Pro Team 1984 and 1985.

Despite never having caught a touchdown pass in a Super Bowl game, Monk's ability to make big catches has been a consistent factor throughout his career.

JERRY RICE

Jerry Rice has made the NFL All-Pro Team each season from 1986 through 1993, and he is still going strong.

JERRY RICE

JERRY RICE HAS AN INCREDIBLE knack for getting to the end zone. But one of his biggest catches for the San Francisco 49ers set up the touchdown for someone else.

The 49ers trailed the Cincinnati Bengals, 16-13, in Super Bowl XXIII. They drove all the way from their own eight-yard line but were still 45 yards from the end zone with barely a minute left in the game. Rice took off and cut toward the middle of the field. Not only did he slip through three defensive backs to catch Joe Montana's pass at the thirty-two-yard line, he ran another 14 yards before he was brought down. Two plays later, the 49ers scored the winning touchdown. Rice, with 11 catches for 215 yards, was named the Super Bowl's Most Valuable Player.

Growing up in Mississippi, Jerry Rice and his brothers helped their father who was a bricklayer. Jerry would stand on scaffolding as his brothers threw bricks—sometimes four at a time—up to him. Catching bricks gave him strong hands that later helped him to catch and hang onto footballs. By helping his father lay bricks, Rice also developed a habit for hard work. He stays in shape after the football season is over, and this off-season conditioning contributes to the fact that he has never missed a game in his career.

Jerry Rice attended Mississippi Valley State in Itta Bena, Mississippi. It wasn't a major college powerhouse but Rice attracted many pro scouts to watch him play. The scouts were impressed with Jerry Rice and had no doubt he would be a star in the NFL. For good measure, Rice would sit with the scouts as they watched films of his games. That way, he could make sure that they didn't miss any of the highlights.

Rice joined the San Francisco 49ers in 1985. He struggled through much of the season, dropping more than his share of passes. He finally hit his stride toward the end of the year. He finished the season with 49 catches for 927 yards and was named Rookie of the Year in the National Football Conference. He followed that up by leading the league in receiving yardage and touchdown catches the next year. Then, in 1987, he set an NFL record with 22 touchdown receptions (despite playing in only twelve games because of a mid-season players' strike).

Jerry Rice has become known both for his spectacular catches and his ability to break away from defenders and pick up more yards after the catch. Rice played on two Super Bowl championship teams. The year after he helped the 49ers beat Cincinnati, he caught three touchdown passes in a 55-10 romp over Denver in Super Bowl XXIV in January 1990.

One of the biggest moments in his career came near the end of 1992. It was a rainy day at Candlestick Park, the 49ers home field, and San Francisco had the game in hand, leading Miami 20-3. But the fans remained for one reason—Jerry Rice. Even though this was only his eighth season in the league, Rice had caught 100 touchdown passes in his career. It was a record he shared—for the time being—with Steve Largent. Then it happened. He broke off the line, headed for the end zone, and grabbed a Steve Young pass for a touchdown. Touchdown catch 101 gave him the career record all to himself.

By the time he retires, Jerry Rice will undoubtedly break many more records. His performance confirms a comment once made about him by former teammate Dwight Clark: "The first time I saw him, he was the best I ever saw."[1]

JERRY RICE

BORN: October 13, 1962.

HIGH SCHOOL: B.L. Moor High School, Crawford, MS.

COLLEGE: Mississippi Valley State.

PRO: San Franscisco 49ers, 1985– .

RECORDS: Most total touchdowns in a career set early in 1994; Most touchdown receptions (118 through 1993); Most touchdown receptions in one season (22 in 1987).

HONORS: NFL All-Pro Team, 1986–1993; Most Valuable Player, Super Bowl XXIII.

Jerry Rice started his NFL career by being named Rookie of the Year. The record numbers of touchdowns and receptions he has say all there is to say about his continuing success.

STERLING SHARPE

IT WAS THE OPENING PLAYOFF GAME following the 1993 season. Sterling Sharpe had already caught two touchdowns in the game, but his Green Bay Packers trailed the Detroit Lions by three points with barely a minute left in the fourth quarter. The Packers were on the Detroit forty-yard line, still out of range of a field goal that could tie the game. But Sharpe and the Packers weren't thinking in terms of a tie. Sterling took off down the right sideline. He slowed down and looked back. Quarterback Brett Favre was under pressure and started to scramble. Sharpe took off, leaving his defender far behind. Favre spotted his favorite receiver running all alone and sailed a long pass downfield. As he crossed the goal line, Sharpe stuck out his hands to make the catch for his third touchdown of the day, this one was a game winner.

Sharpe has a reputation for using his speed and strength to run for extra yards after the reception. He's been called "a top receiver after the catch." Although his playoff catch against the Lions was on a sideline pattern, he's better known for going into heavy traffic in the middle of the field.

Sterling Sharpe was born in Chicago and lived there until he was seven. At that time, his parents sent him, along with a sister and a brother (his brother, Shannon Sharpe, is also a receiver in the NFL), to live with his grandmother in Glennville, Georgia. The Sharpes felt that their children would be better off in a small Georgia town rather than growing up in a city like Chicago, where violence and drugs were a greater problem. Sharpe later said that moving to Georgia "was the best thing that ever happened to me."[1]

In addition to playing running back, quarterback, and

Although he has been in the NFL only since 1988, Sterling Sharpe has been named an All-Pro four times.

STERLING SHARPE

linebacker at Glennview High, he was also a member of the basketball and track teams. He went to college at South Carolina, where he set school records with 169 career receptions and 2,497 receiving yards. He also had a record, since broken, with 17 career touchdown catches.

Sharpe was drafted by Green Bay and made an immediate impact on the Packers. He started all sixteen games for them his rookie season of 1988 and caught 55 passes. The next season, he led the league with 90 receptions, the first Packer to do that since Don Hutson in 1945. He also broke Hutson's team records for receptions and receiving yards (Sharpe had 1,423) in a season.

His second-year statistics were so impressive that some people wondered if he'd ever be able to top them. In 1992, Sharpe and new Packer quarterback Brett Favre teamed up as one of the top passing tandems in the league.

In the final game of the 1992 season, Sharpe caught a short pass from Favre. It was his 107th reception of the season, breaking the NFL record that Art Monk had set eight years earlier. Sharpe's record would not last that long, however; it would be broken the very next year. The person who broke it was Sterling Sharpe. In 1993 Sharpe caught 112 passes to shatter his own record. In setting the new mark, he also became the only player to ever catch more than 100 passes in one season, two years in a row.

Although he's been in the NFL only since 1988, Sterling Sharpe has been an All-Pro four times. He's caught the most passes, 501, of any player in history in his first six seasons in the league, and is making his mark as one of the greatest receivers ever.

"No receiver possesses the fearlessness that has marked Sharpe's career," wrote one sportswriter. "Sharpe will take licks and dish them out as well."[2]

STERLING SHARPE

BORN: April 6, 1965.

HIGH SCHOOL: Glenville, GA.

COLLEGE: University of South Carolina.

PRO: Green Bay Packers, 1988– .

RECORDS: Most receptions in season (112 in 1993).

HONORS: NFL All-Pro Team, 1989, 1992, 1993.

In his first six seasons in the NFL, Sharpe has caught the most passes of any player in history.

LYNN SWANN

Lynn Swann was named the NFL Man of the Year in 1981. He has remained involved in football as a sports commentator.

LYNN SWANN

HE WAS AS GRACEFUL AS his last name suggests—and just as acrobatic. Lynn Swann studied ballet and performed gymnastics as he grew up. Later he used those skills on the football field, leaping high to snag passes and thrill fans. He's remembered for soaring in the big games. And Swann played in plenty of them. As a member of the Pittsburgh Steelers from 1974 through 1982, Swann played in four Super Bowls. The Steelers won all four, thanks in large part to Lynn Swann.

Because of a concussion he suffered in the AFC Championship Game, no one was sure if Swann would even play in Super Bowl X against Dallas. But play he did, and Swann turned in the greatest receiving performance ever seen in a Super Bowl.

With the Steelers trailing, 7-0, in the first quarter, Swann streaked down the sideline. A Cowboy defender stayed with him and they both jumped for the pass. Swann's leaping ability payed off. He grabbed the ball and used his grace to bring both feet down in bounds. It was a 32-yard gain and it set up the tying touchdown for Pittsburgh.

Later, the Steelers were stuck deep in their own territory in the second quarter. Terry Bradshaw threw a long pass to Swann. It seemed to be floating beyond Swann's reach, but he lunged, got his hands on it, and juggled it briefly before getting control for a 53-yard gain.

Then in the fourth quarter, the Steelers were ahead, 15-10. They faced a third down on their own thirty-six-yard line and were in danger of having to give the ball back to the Cowboys. Bradshaw sent Swann on a long pattern down the middle. The quarterback got his pass away just before he was hit by a blitzing Cowboy. Swann caught the ball on the run at the five-yard line and glided into the end zone. His touchdown proved to be the game winner as Pittsburgh held on for a 21-17 win. In all, Swann caught four passes for 161 yards and was named the Most Valuable Player of the game.

Swann came to the Steelers after an outstanding college career at the University of Southern California. He was a three-year starter with the Trojans and an All-American wide receiver his senior season. Just as he would later excel in Super Bowls, Swann had a couple of fine games in the two Rose Bowls in which he played.

As a first-round draft pick for the Steelers in 1974, Swann spent most of his rookie season returning punts and serving as a backup receiver to Ron Shanklin. By the end of the year, however, he got more playing time on offense and even scored the winning touchdown in that season's AFC Championship Game against the Oakland Raiders.

He made the starting lineup in his second year in Pittsburgh, capping the season with his memorable performance in Super Bowl X. He had another great performance in his next Super Bowl three years later, also against the Dallas Cowboys. Swann caught seven passes for 124 yards and a touchdown. Swann would play in another Super Bowl—the very next year—and catch another touchdown, this one a 47-yard bomb from Terry Bradshaw.

Swann played nine seasons with Pittsburgh, leading the Steelers in pass receptions six times. By the time he retired in 1982, he held several team career receiving records.

Swann is best remembered in Pittsburgh, as well as the rest of the country, for the way he finished off a few of his seasons. Highlight films of Super Bowls feature plenty of footage of Lynn Swann, a man who saved his biggest plays for the biggest games.

LYNN SWANN

BORN: March 7, 1952.

HIGH SCHOOL: Serra High School, Foster City, CA.

COLLEGE: University of Southern California.

PRO: Pittsburgh Steelers, 1974–1983.

HONORS: Most Valuable Player, Super Bowl X; All-Pro, 1977, 1978.

Swann was named Most Valuable Player in Super Bowl X in 1975. He demonstrates his graceful moves as he makes this touchdown catch.

NOTES BY CHAPTER

Introduction
1. John Devaney, *Star Pass Receivers of the NFL* (New York: Random House, 1972), p. 8.

Lance Alworth
1. John Devaney, *Star Pass Receivers of the NFL* (New York: Random House, 1972), p. 78.
2. Ibid., p. 88.

Raymond Berry
1. David Porter, ed. *Biographical Dictionary of American Sports: Football* (New York: Greenwood Press, 1987), p. 42.

Elroy Hirsch
1. Stuart Leuthner, *Iron Men: Bucko, Crazylegs, and the Boys Recall the Golden Days of Professional Football* (New York: Doubleday, 1988), p 173.
2. Don R. Smith, *NFL Pro Football Hall of Fame All-Time Greats* (New York: Gallery Books, 1988), p. 90.
3. Joseph Hession, *Rams: Five Decades of Football* (San Francisco: Foghorn Press, 1987), p. 37.
4. Ibid., p. 38.

Don Hutson
1. David L. Porter, ed. *Biographical Dictionary of American Sports: Football* (New York: Greenwood Press, 1987), p. 281.
2. Richard Whittingham, *What a Game They Played: An Inside Look at the Golden Era of Pro Football* (New York: Simon & Schuster, Inc., 1984), pp. 126-127.
3. Porter, p. 282.

Steve Largent
1. Jill Lieber "The Catch of the Day." *Sports Illustrated* (October 20, 1986), p. 48.

Don Maynard
1. John Devaney, *Star Pass Receivers of the NFL* (New York: Random House, 1972), pp. 133-134.

2. Ibid., p. 130.

Art Monk
1. "If You Throw It, He Will Catch It." *Time* (October 26, 1992), p. 26.

Jerry Rice
1. J. Edward Evans, *Jerry Rice: Touchdown Talent* (Minneapolis: Lerner Publications, 1993), p. 8.

Sterling Sharpe
1. George Castle, "Leader of the Pack." *Sport* (September 1993), p. 81.

2. Ibid., p. 82.

Lynn Swann
No notes.

INDEX